RUSH HOUR

RUSH HOUR

Kevin FitzPatrick

Kevin FitzPatrick

MIDWEST VILLAGES & VOICES

Some of these poems have appeared in the following magazines and anthologies: *The Alley, ArtWord Quarterly, Blossoms & Blizzards* (Pegasus Prose), *A Coloring Book of Poetry for Adults, Volume 2* (Vanilla Press), *disturbed guillotine, Family Times, Java Junkie, Labor and the Post-Industrial Age* (Pig Iron Press), *Lake Street Review, Loonfeather, Mankato Poetry Review, The Next Parish Over* (New Rivers Press), *North Coast Review, The North Stone Review, Ophelia's Pale Lilies, The Pikestaff Forum, PinchPenny, The Selby-Lake Bus* (Lake Street Review Press), *Sidewalks, The Summit Avenue Express, Thirteen, Waterways,* and *Wide Open.*

Midwest Villages & Voices
Post Office Box 40214
Saint Paul, Minnesota 55104

First edition
Library of Congress Catalog Card Number: 96-76209
ISBN 0-935697-08-X
Designed by J. B. Sisson
Cover photograph by Tina Marie Blomer
Manufactured in the United States of America

For Tina

CONTENTS

ONE: RUDE LIFE

TWO: PEDALING BACK

ONE

RUDE LIFE

RUDE LIFE

The asphalt's wet but free of snow at last,
and breathless boys contend at basketball,
trying to finish one more game real fast
despite a father's loud persistent call.
An easy shot blocked and the slick ball sails
over the soggy yard to plop in crud.
"I quit!" the chaser groans, and all agree,
scattering home on dark familiar trails.
School clothes smudged, tennis shoes oozing with mud—
one will catch hell for tearing his pants knee.

Across the street from the abandoned game,
gardens and yards are crusted with gray snow.
The late March sun's a distant placid flame
as ice forts still could stop a snowball's blow.
I enter a small house on that chilled side
for Tim O'Connell's wake. His coffin's set
where I recall his mother's favorite chair.
A boyhood friend: makeup and lights can't hide
the weight he lost. I pause in front, then let
a bunch of children by. They squirm and stare.

Outside, a bouncing sound, a slow drumbeat:
two boys who must have gulped their meals are back.
Rivals at horse, one yells, "You slimeball cheat!"
for launching a jump shot way past the crack.
Rude life across the street stirs loud and clear,
as mourners kneel. Leaving, I think how Tim
would have laughed knowing that our loose games, fought
so long ago, go on. These shouts I hear
resound tonight as holy as a hymn,
recalling Tim's trick pass I never caught.

DAGGER'S GIFT

Dagger arrives in a gray suit and tie
as if he's here to lead a choral group.
Forty now, filling out, his face and stomach
paunchy, he says in class he goes by "Dagger,"
but if we call at work—a clothing store,
a real good job, he adds—ask for Cornell.

Where's that lean fiery figure on his album,
defiantly poised atop a snowy bench,
blues harp and wine thawing the ice-clogged river?
Dagger could blow one hot harmonica,
tormented notes, storm wail of rage and pain.
I signed up for the class to learn from him.

"You're Dagger?" asks a student coming late.
Unmiffed, he hands the guy a course outline
and list of songs to listen to and try
from "Jug Band Waltz" to "Bottle Up and Go."
The puzzled student asks to just take notes:
he's busy now with work and holidays.

"Just notes? I blew my brains out learning harp!
I begged Blind Snaker Smith to let me tape
his 'Snakebite Moan.' Then days inside my room,
slowing my reel-to-reel to catch each riff.
'I've got it down!' I roared when I came out.
'You do,' my roommate said, 'thank God, you do.'"

Now smoothly drawing a harmonica
from his breast pocket like a fine cigar,
he snaps, "Let's move," and runs a funky scale.

THE BOXER WITH THE WITHERED ARM

He removes the robe.
His right arm
hangs
a short bone,
a gloved claw,
as his left
bulges
a blacksmith's arm.
Here
in this roped space
no one jokes
of cripples swimming
in circles
or cheers
now
for an underdog.

BEARING ARMS

As she emerges tired from late-night work,
a man approaches on her homeward path.
She tightens purse and packages. "You jerk,"
she thinks, "don't dare touch me." He feels her wrath
and understands unease on a dark street.
He crosses over so they do not meet.

In bed she dreams of the endangered swan
wildlife officials struggled hard to hatch.
But now a furtive mink, when they have gone,
slithers through a pipe to gnaw its scrawny catch
until a feathery mess is all that's left,
the senseless ruins of an instinctive theft.

Her bullets hit low on the practice range.
Her handgun teacher's quick pinpoint advice
to strike the heart: Level the sights and change
to a firm grip. She does and bull's-eyes twice.
For weeks she ponders purchasing a gun,
uncertain whether she could kill someone.

One night she hurries across her lawn, then halts.
Beyond the driveway light a stranger's pausing.
"What good's a locked-up gun if he assaults?"
she thinks. "Maybe he's dense to the fear he's causing?"
Until he goes, she stays behind the fence
with her small barking dog and her gut sense.

PLANE CRASH

What really happened:
the DC-10 had entered
the cosmic equivalent
of a well-scrubbed kitchen
where a muscular inhabitant panicking
at a large silver bug
buzzing the blue ceiling
struck it overhand
like a tennis ball,
swatting it out and in
again to this world of hard facts
where a few stunned passengers
saw green,
smelled fresh-cut grass,
and, giddy and running,
called in unison,
"Are we alive? Are we alive?"

OPENING THE DOOR

I will tell you this:
It happened some time ago.
We were in a car
at the edge of the city.
I will not identify the others,
but one friend had a pistol.
He became a Green Beret
and then a survivalist.
I am telling you this
because that friend
has disappeared.

This is enough.
Unlike the politician guilty as hell,
bellowing his innocence on the capitol steps,
I am ashamed.
My friend who pulled the trigger
and then confessed to a priest
does not recall that night,
as if we were shooting at bats
in an abandoned barn. Even then I, reeling,
nearly shot his head off
as the bats scattered and swooped.

I would tell you more,
but even if I altered my voice
and hunched behind a screen,
we would be identified.
My friend has not called
since I asked if his four sons
pull any of our old stuff.

I tell you this much
but promise
if the man stops again late at night
to kick at my fence over and over,
then idle long seconds behind the wheel,

his interior light brightly on,
I will open the door
of that familiar-looking car
and answer fully.

NORTHBOUND LANE

If it was light out,
the day staff would have seen him trip
and pulled him from the trench of snow.
And even if the reporter had been drinking,
a shopper would have gathered his hat.

As if he's a swimmer going down
in steep waves of snow,
he raises one arm to a passerby
who, seeing a human figure flat
in the middle of the northbound lane,
the newspaper's brown building dimly lit,
steps cautiously out
of his long day and stares,
then thinks, "The cops'll handle it."

Hoping he doesn't get run over
or freeze, the reporter,
his ankle badly broken,
recalls a story he once wrote:
a man crushed to death,
trapped at dawn in a dumpster
where he had sought shelter and sleep.
His screams were stifled
by the garbage truck's hydraulic whine.

"He wanted to be a writer,"
the man's brother had told him.
"He wasn't what you'd think."

OUT OF THE DEPTHS

Seventy or so,
a purple-haired woman,
peering over the driver's wheel
like a periscope,
shifts and blows forty-
miles-an-hour
of slush and grit.

As she surfaces, I leap
to a dry objective curb.
Her front bumper sticker proclaims,
IN SEARCH OF THE ETERNAL BUZZ.

From the rearview mirror
of her pink mint-condition
'57 Chevy swings
a serene male religious figure
wildly by his neck.

As she descends,
a final message heralds,
GOD IS COMING AND SHE IS PISSED.

WHAT FEARS THEY HAD

With trucks and buses blasting by
a foot or two away from them,
I watched uneasily as she rolled
backward on skates to the curb's edge,

then tugged herself forward by just
a finger in her boyfriend's belt
to whisper something in his ear
that made the two of them laugh hard.

When the light changed from red to green,
I wondered if what fears they had
were rarer—lions and tigers down
in the dark basement's furnace room.

FACTORY DISCLAIMER

Our motorcycles are not made
for use as musical instruments.

CLEARING OF THE SITE

"Much of the new construction in downtown Saint Paul has occurred where parking lots existed from earlier clearing of the site. I think we have been most sensitive to the architectural value, the beauty and charm of our older structures."

—From a letter from an elected official

January 5, 1990

Wisely, politicians don't show up
at demolitions of historic buildings.
It would be suicide
to wave from the crane's cab
as the wrecking ball bowls
into the belly of a building—
a blow felt in the guts
of all of us this afternoon,
disgruntled strangers
protesting as ineffectually
as the peanut gallery on "Howdy Doody"
when Clarabell with his seltzer bottle
sneaks up on Buffalo Bob
despite our pleas to look out.
We'd be better off letter writing.
I called the mayor this morning.
A trained voice transferred my rage
to the Office of Information and Complaint,
which read me a news clip
as if it were a bedtime story:
"Nicols Dean and Gregg Building...
elegant warehouse...
Classical Revival style...
massive stone basement...
pressed creamy-brown brick...
capped by decorative metal cornice...
architectural landmark...
when it's gone, it's gone forever..."
"Well, why are they tearing it down?"
"You mean it's not down yet?"

January 12, 1990
An aerial view presents
a heap in one corner
where a towering red crane
launches a black claw
leisurely, like the rope
a child swings on over a lake,
before it drops down
to drag a load of twisted rubble
a yellow bulldozer dumps
into a long green truck
as a man in orange rain pants
scurries over the remains,
shooting water from a gray hose
to squelch dust that might
disrupt this sandbox scene,
clouding downtown with irritants
until citizens really grumble
what the hell is going on.

January 19, 1990
A blue road grader smooths
a flat profitable space,
which in a year or so transforms
into an open stage for politicians,
smiling beneath white hard hats,
to ply with gold-plated shovels
the malleable soil of memory.

LESSONS

In our high-school lunchroom I let him be.
Grabbing a handful of McMillan's chips
would spark a leaping in-my-face response
as if I seized a lion's bloody prey.
But when Mac had his fill of salt and grease,
he'd flick the bag toward me. "Here, finish these."
My formal lessons are dim like faded chalk.
I'd hesitate to raise my hand today
for lithosphere, the capital of Maine,
ablative, irony, Nonpartisan League,
though I recall our principal, Father Shea,
lecturing us: "Real men will kiss their moms."
"Failures in life weren't active in their schools."
"Go when you've got to go. Don't hold it in."
"Taylor and Burton will be broiled in hell."
Those movie stars while filming *Cleopatra*
so maddened Father Shea one Lenten mass
he put his sermon down, and we stirred up
to hear his thundering on grown-up sins,
which I enjoyed some years ahead, but now,
settled with a devoted wife, I'm wise
to store those memories as if in sealed
moisture-proof boxes on a basement shelf.
I will recall one splendid afternoon,
a hot sun-shower day, my lovely friend—
where is she now?—revealed how covering
grilled cheese sandwiches quickly melts the cheese,
and then—though I was old enough and should
have known—she taught me how to pour a beer,
tilting the glass sideways to thwart the foam.
With that I'll follow Father's parting words:
"Keep your ears open and your big mouth shut."

NEIGHBORS

"My neighbors watch," he says,
"watch me come, watch me go."
A short thin black man,
sixty or so,
in front of me at the checkout,
wearing a Twins cap and a gray
United Auto Workers jacket,
coaxes his purchase, a case
of Old Milwaukee in cans,
into the largest brown bag
the popcorn-eating clerk offers.

The man had quipped earlier,
"Makes you want to quit drinking,"
when I was pondering prices
down a long aisle of various whiskeys.
Now I wonder if I caught his drift
as I remark to him about neighbors,
"I don't like my neighbors either
seeing me bring alcohol home."

"But with my neighbors"—he smiles
as he flips the bagged case over
and digs through to grip its handle—
"I get too much company."

Leaning sideways,
he lugs his suitcase out,
the coveted contents only partially concealed.
I think of my neighbors and his,
how I barely know mine,
how uneasy I'd be
drinking with them.

AFTER THE BURGLARY

Tougher locks, the police advise:
dead bolt,
double key.

We have wooden doors front and back,
doors that hard kicks
could crack open.

Saint Jude,
Saint Anthony of Padua,
patron saints of the desperate,

whose holy cards I sneaked each game
into the thigh pads
of my football pants,

pray for us.

THINNING SHADE

With sixteen years before I can retire,
I'll stick it out as long as there's a job.
And that's what frightens me: a span of time
from first grade through a college education.
I'll listen up, this round, and learn my math,
then choose a specialty in medicine,
at sixty start a new career as thrilled
as one who's finally free of family care
or extricated from an odious job.

In truth I see myself in thinning shade,
no more ambitious than a fattening squirrel
as leaves begin to fall. Scrounging beneath
a hanging feeder, I would pounce on seeds
that sparrows brush aside in fussy haste,
until my mouth is bulging far beyond
hunger or any future winter need.

CLEANS * DISINFECTS * DEODORIZES

Although we share the household cleaning chores—
I usually do the bathroom and the vacuuming—
it took me all this time living with her
to comprehend the concentrated power
that's activated washing kitchen floors.
Now mop in hand, I revel in "It's wet.
You can't come in. Don't try. Don't even try.
Go out the front to get your beer downstairs."
I'm suddenly a puffed-up righteous troll
slowing, diverting the rash rush-hour commuters
to dark side roads and trembling wooden bridges.
Annoyed, she says, "At least I'll never snap
'Why don't you tell me when you do the floor!'
You'll learn you do the kitchen when you can."

ARE YOU ALL RIGHT?

Surprised she's home from work early today,
I enter warily. Her car outside,
the mail not taken in, a TV tray
tipped by her winter coat—something's cockeyed.
I draw my words like guns: "Are you all right?"
Upstairs a mound in bed. I tap. "What's wrong?"
Her whispering "A cold" relieves my fright,
calms me like notes of a familiar song.
As if her sickness were more than a flat tire,
she shakes her head. "Why me? It isn't fair."
Outside our window on an icy wire
mourning doves coo that spring is in the air.
Pajamas, matted hair, her sure voice hoarse:
forced penitent as her illness runs its course.

SOARING CRANE KARATE

Crowding against the counter, teenaged boys
plead to just let them touch the throwing star
that's under glass. By law it's rubber coated.
"I'd sharpen up those points," one says. "How far
can it be thrown?" another asks the clerk.
A mother in this crew questions her son,
"But what would you do with a thing like that?"
"Jeez, Mom, they're cool to have. They're really fun."

A black-belt teacher in a tailored gi
has his arm in a sling. A student here,
a football star, he says, had kicked him hard
though both of them wore padded sparring gear.
"Hey, could you kill someone with your bare hands?"
"You really teach guys on the Vikings team?"
The black belt answers like a talk-show host,
breezy, with quips, at ease in their esteem.

I'm in the way. I buy *Karate Basics*,
the book I'll use to train at home—kicks, blocks,
hand strikes—but I don't dream like an old boxer
that I'll be quick and tough with fists like rocks.
I'm forty-three and sit all day at work.
I studied karate many years ago
and see myself in faces here, but now
I mark inertia as my dreaded foe.

LAKE SUPERIOR VACATION

Reaching the white-pine peak, we eat our lunch,
our bodies demanding food and drink, unlike
work at my desk, where coffee will suffice.
Water, trail mix, cheese, bagels fuel our hike.
While pondering where the lake turns into sky,
I hear a nearby climber's sharp phone call,
his curses echoing a deal gone sour.
If I were him, I'd hike a shopping mall.

At camp the startling hot June afternoon
is cool in our screened tent. While Tina reads,
I watch a bumblebee amid white blossoms,
my thoughts alighting where the insect leads.
Getting away, time off, a good brain dusting,
the word "vacation" thrills me like a shout
"Oasis!" after many hardpan months.
And there's a silver-beaded waterspout.

Tina looks up. "How can you just sit there
without a book?" "I think I finally see"—
I nod profoundly—"an elemental truth:
what 'busy' means in 'busy as a bee.'"
What's more, I read too much at work and home.
Out here I want my thoughts to casually flow.
"Will you check in for calls?" a colleague asked.
Politely I conveyed to him "Hell, no."

AT A GREAT LAKES LIGHTHOUSE HISTORIC SITE

Their nerve or recklessness amazes me.
Before the high illuminating light

warned ships away from imminent jagged rock,
before good sense and government resources

built this lighthouse of steadfast native stone
to bear the huff and puff of centuries,

tough weathered captains and their crews who sailed
the busy shipping lanes that cross these lakes

long knew in fog or unexpected storm
their cherished compasses were often tricked

by metal properties in the looming cliffs,
veering their crafts from reckoned ports to horror,

but on tight schedules, carrying their wealth
like buoyant cornucopias, ships sped on.

Looking for work that would have fit me here,
I see myself stationed within the bright

and level lighthouse service workshop, tools
hung neatly over high turned-legged tables.

Replacing prisms in the Fresnel lens,
I wear a pressed shop coat, wool vest, and tie

and concentrate on my fine-finger task
as closely as a Lake Superior captain

plunged in a storm but piloting his ship
with savvy by the brilliant sweeping light.

INTO THE FIRE

A woman on the front porch shouted, "Fire!"
He froze at first. "There's people caught inside,"
she urged. He grabbed a shovel from his truck.
"In back, in back, please run, oh run," she cried.

He tried the knob. The outer door was locked.
He tried the knob again, as green-black smoke
crowded against the glass inside. He smashed
his shovel through. The window partially broke.

Ah hell, just kick the damn door in. He found
a naked woman heaped on the entry floor,
a boy in blue pajamas clinging to her.
He hauled her by the armpits through the door,

her arms red gashes from the glass he'd shattered.
He stretched her on a bench, but she slumped down
dazed, moaning, as he darted for the boy,
his nostrils blackened like a grotesque clown,

and lifted him away toward cleaner air.
He breathed into his mouth but got a groan,
"Uh-uh," as if he didn't want to breathe,
as if he'd just as soon be left alone,

as if each breath were like his mother's voice
calling him home from an amusement park
full of fun games, free rides, and clear blue skies,
calling him back to the cramped, gagging dark.

Nor did the passerby who rescued them
want to go back. He'd done what he could do.
Where was the woman who had sent him here?
Where were the others? Where was the fire crew?

Next door an Asian man with a white beard
watched like a judge awaiting one last try

from this young man to pass a crucial test.
But he, as sirens neared, let out a sigh.

That night in dream he's there before the fire:
The mother walks around the kitchen nude,
washing and drying dishes. Smoke begins
seeping from a bedroom where she has shooed

her husband and two boys until she's done.
She glances out and sees him wave and call
to her. And, smiling, she unlocks the door,
and, checking room by room, they save them all.

"First off, I'm puzzled. How'd the back door break?"
the fire inspector asked. "Elaine told me
she's sure it wasn't locked. The duplex owner
wants her to pay for damaged property."

"The door was locked. I kicked until it cracked."
"Where were Elaine and Seth when you got in?"
"Against the door. I cut her with the glass."
"And did the entry smoke increase or thin?"

"I couldn't tell." "But did you see an arm
a few feet in from where you brought them out?"
"I didn't look. I just saw smoke. I'm not
a hero. Anyway, some others were about.

I did what I could do, but now I read
that Gail, the one who called me off the street,
claims it was she who pulled them from the fire.
The story's told as an amazing feat."

"That's strange. I missed the paper yesterday.
You did a lot. Your average citizen
usually doesn't. Hey, I'll call the *Star*."
He never heard from the inspector again.

TWO

PEDALING BACK

PEDALING BACK

Home's so far,
I hope I don't have to pedal back again.
Dad could beat him.
He used to box and wears sunglasses,
but Coach can yell and smokes cigars.
I'm not chicken—it's swelling.
The fullback stepped on it when he fumbled.
Coach says, "Go home, gutless."
Dad says, "The hell with him. Ride back there right now."
Then Coach says, "Get lost, or you're through."
I'm not chicken,
but I hope I don't have to pedal back again.
These hills are hard one-handed.

IN MY MOTHER'S VOICE

One thing I really missed
when they had all died
was that there was no one
to tell the little things to,
the things about you kids.
Oh, I had my sisters and the neighbors,
but they had their kids.
There was no one who cared anymore
the way your grandparents did
to hear all the little things
about school
or paper routes
or what the girls wore on Easter.
I missed that.

BREAKFAST DISHES

Her children at her constantly, she feels
like the scarecrow in *The Wizard of Oz*:
out of nowhere a son flies by and steals
a beak of straw so fast she cannot pause
to think for just one second if she ate
her breakfast yet. The morning's been a blur.
And now her oldest daughter tells her straight
she'd rather not be seen in church with her.
Where are those nuns, she wonders, who instilled
in her throughout her college years that mothering
a flock like hers would make her feel fulfilled
in God. How dare her daughter call her smothering.
She imagines sisters back from morning prayers,
ending their fast with tea and cream éclairs.

SUPPOSEDLY WHEN MY FATHER WAS YOUNG

Before I will believe you, Uncle,

I will need a wireless mike, a powerful one,
that can thrust back through decades of my father's truth
to transmit evidence indicting him and his friends,
placing them around a huge oak table
Sunday mornings in the back of Stewart's Café,

a mike alert to a clink of what you say are whiskey glasses,
to loud last slurps,
to their crowd of footsteps leaving over the red brick
  street.

Before I will believe you, Uncle,

I will need a wireless mike, a tiny one,
that can tug to my father's lapel like an invisible leash
to transmit evidence indicting him and his friends
rushing up church steps as if propelled by a huge oak
  table
Sunday mornings swirling in the back of Stewart's Café,

a mike alive to the grate of clearing throats,
to my father's bass voice amidst a high-mass hosanna,
to a devout choir bluff above the altar of Saint Thomas,

before I will believe you, Uncle.

A PHOTOGRAPH OF A FAMOUS PERSON, AGED ELEVEN, WITH CLASSMATES, 1887

Were these police lineup expressions,
somber as the girls' long gray dresses
and the boys' black coats and stern collars,
the style of that day,
or did they sense we would be scanning
back for the whereabouts of only one?

And would we appreciate this smile,
the jaw jutting toward the nearest exit,
or shun him as too cocky
if we were among these serious children,
troubled by a vague light
that now haloes his illustrious head?

STAYING AFTER SCHOOL FOR TALKING

You know, Ms. Stricker, you could stop
this after-school martyrdom
by letting us during class fill our mouths with gum,
a peanut-butter cup, and Tootsie Pop.
Our constant chattering would easily end,
and like a cherry drop
you would be our friend.

BLOODY NOSES NOT ENOUGH

The word's out all over school:
Three o'clock! In the lot!
Klogs pushed Ted in class!

And Klogs will beat him—he's a big kid—
though Ted's tough and won't quit
till a broke tooth wins excuse
from the close, enclosing crowd.

GUNS DON'T KILL PEOPLE

He bashes the barrel against a rock
with the fury of a torturer impotent to extract
a sensible confession.

His son who hunts pheasant with him,
his son who's used a shotgun a lot,
his son who always does a safety check.

He was not to be in the house without adults,
he was not to unlock the cabinet,
he was not to get into the shells.

If his friend had not been right there, stroking the cat,
if his friend had not leaned forward that second,
if his son's finger had not slipped.

SPLIT HOCKEY STICK

It is almost dark. He can no longer see his running friends, though he hears their laughing screams far up the alley. Above his head his red stocking cap is glowing fainter. It is a last ember in an apple tree that has been charred by winter.

He can't go home without it. But they threw it there. Still, she would send him right back before he could take off an overshoe. It would be darker. But he has tried almost everything: jumping and climbing, shaking the tree, and snowballs. If he were only taller. Still, he is too tall to count on tears and too tall to count on a giant who would stop and from way on the sidewalk swat it to him with a huge mittened hand.

He will be happy for anyone walking slowly home through snow in the dark, anyone a couple of inches taller, who would put down a lunch bucket or shopping bag to help him. Until then he will continue, though his face is getting redder, trying, though it hurts his toes, to kick loose a split hockey stick that is long enough but seems stuck to the earth with cement.

A GATHERING IN THE SOUTH HIGH PARKING LOT

Guys in jean jackets and smudged pants are slouching
near, but never on, a '73 Chevy,
the fastest car in school, and its canary yellow
custom-painted by Kosmoski at his House of Kolor.

Their chewing-gum mouths are moving
up and down together,
enjoying an orange flavor of Florida some Easter,
beating the super stocks at Daytona.

STRAWBERRY MALTS

Way back at the other end of the lunchroom
they are eating together for the first time
in the middle of an empty table, its long yellow length
shooting from their sides like airplane wings.
He bought two strawberry malts today, while she
brought a bag lunch of ham sandwiches and Fritos.

Way up tables and tables near the milk line
his buddies are really horsing around,
fixing each other's arms and legs to tables and chairs
with masking tape swiped from printing class.
They would not admit they are thinking of him,
though they've already given her a nickname.

TOWN AND COUNTRY GOLF CLUB

My last year caddying I butted heads
with the new caddy master, Patrick Quinn.
I was too young for a good summer job
but aging quick to the pep talks he'd spin:

"Gentlemen, pride and excellence, not money,
should be your goals as caddies, as in life."
I laughed: "You mean no pay for the hours here
waiting around." Quinn's look was like a knife.

In late June, Mrs. Wills, who lived near us,
hired me at a dollar twenty-five an hour.
A master portrait painter in her sixties,
she'd let her yard become more weed than flower.

Two days a week I'd dig and hack and clip,
revealing roses, lilies, geraniums,
while Mrs. Wills would stroll the cobbled path,
especially pleased by blue delphiniums.

My father roared like the MGM lion
because I'd stopped caddying and been cut.
"Damn it, you need to pay high-school tuition.
You'll be back on tomorrow. Case is shut!"

The next day Quinn announced my mother'd called,
inciting jeers and then a shoving scene.
I was to come each day and stay till four.
I did as told. Next year I'd be sixteen.

WHAT YOUR WAITING KNOWS

You got me mad,
and I'm never coming up.
I'm going to stay down forever.
You might as well go.
I won a ribbon, you know,
in a water carnival once
for holding my breath the longest.

You keep sitting calmly on the dock
though my splash like a hasty bus
slopped your blouse and hair,

and don't think I need you
or that there's nothing to do
here under the dock:
countless bullheads crowd near,
and sunfish swim to me
and nibble my feet,

but your long white legs
continue swaying slowly
in the water above.

Easing my armlock around
the cold slimy post,
I burst
upward,
realizing what your waiting knows:
I must come up
though I may hold my breath longer
than you or others.
I must come up
even if I had a tank of air.

You reach for me.
I breathe you.

DOWNTIME

Grass, elm, oak, pine—
this green expanse of lawn,
as endangered as a hardwood forest,
has framed the college for a century.

Developers press to build a medical tower,
to decipher codes of cancerous cells,
and multi-tiered parking ramps
so little downtime elapses.

Students could lounge in the library,
professors contemplate in the chapel.
Lovers who stroll this tranquil ground
could schedule time on the jogging track.

YOUR TELEPHONE CALL

I'm fine
or at least okay.
You ask for more,
what I've been doing,
why I'm home,
as if I'm a favorite show
you've been unable to watch,
and when I ask
what you've been doing,
how you are,
in a house I've never seen,
with a man I've never met,
your voice is far away,
as if you're busy
sweeping,
running water
in a distant room
out of hearing.

STARTING OVER

My dream is simply to go,
with the door wide open, the TV blaring,
my money scattered across the dresser,

grabbing nothing,
not even consulting a map,

destination unknown.
Let the landlord think
I've gone for cigarettes.

At rent time he'll remove the remains
to a locker in the cellar.

WANDERER'S PUNCH

The bartender brings another,
a red bubbling liquid
in a clumsy bowl of a glass.
"It's a foul drink," I tell him.
He tells me, "It's the Wanderer's Punch,"
and points to the end of the bar,
to a blur of smoke and faces.
Did she send it?

At closing time he brings a wagon, once blue,
loads six untouched drinks,
adds a seventh, and says,
"Keep the wagon."
Which one was she?

Pulling the wagon home,
I think of her,
the beautiful woman,
the fulfilling love
palmists keep promising me.
Already I have doubts:
the earmuffs,
this leisure suit,
now these ridiculous drinks.
Thinking of her,
I take a long drink,
thinking of uncertain gifts
certain to come.

SOCIAL DANCE I

Beamy as the high-school pep club,
who must have painted them,
bright orange tigers
roam across the yellow walls.
My dreams like my wet winter shoes
are removed at the door.
This is no place for romance.

The gray custodian who unlocked
this low fluorescent lunchroom
has left hints of this:
spills of chocolate milk
splotching white tables,
an occasional Tater Tot
dotting the tile floor.

My hands dampen.
I'm the only man here,
but we swing to "Pistol-Packin' Mama"
over and over and over
until I stumble to a chair weary
as the one riding horse
at a small carnival.

I should have taken "Beginning Harmonica":
"Be the hit of every party,"
playing "Dixie" and "The Marines' Hymn."
Still, I'm here in my socks,
and those shriveled shoes by the door
won't get me anywhere.
Let's cha-cha, shall we?

UNEMPLOYMENT OFFICE

I am here to receive my compensation. I find my file immediately. A blue paper clip like an honor-society pin proclaims it amid masses of manila folders heaped across the office tables. Others must dig for theirs.

Blue is the color of professionals. Others envy me as they scuff to the job viewers for hours of detailed descriptions of manual work, hard work, like tile scrubbing and bottle breaking.

With the shortage in blue positions, we have received new viewers. I am here early this week. My screen is showing the Los Angeles Philharmonic in color, Zubin Mehta conducting.

Just now a bulletin deafens the music and the picture of a Mozart piano concerto: a news flash from Seventh and Marquette. A couple of shriveled characters, one a woman in a blue crumpled business suit, the other a man in a black uniform, boots and cap like a chauffeur or the secret police, are seizing passersby and yelling, "Capitalism must end now!" The two push through my job viewer in fine color, their shouting teeth yellow and gray.

The concerto resumes.

AFTER READING PLATO ALL SUMMER

Something about a would-be scholar
needing a good memory
is all I remember.

READING ABOUT COCKROACHES

The only favorable thing,
according to the encyclopedia,
that can be said about cockroaches
is that they eat bedbugs.
Those black ants would have burped
hearing this the other morning
as they flipped a roach onto its back
and tugged it, a reluctant rowboat of meat,
into a forest of grass and weeds.

More can be said for cockroaches:
they're not pests like mosquitoes
on sweltering nights when I'm nearing sleep
or flies who treat me like a cow
on beaches I've driven miles for,
and when I come home late,
finding them loose on the floor,
they don't loll in the light like stunned
adulterers in unzipped clothes,
wallowing in intimate germs,
but already are moving,
quick brown tanks retreating
where only gas can snuff them out.

Still, they rattle me,
and I continue reading
that cockroaches existed before humans
and that diseases cling to their legs—
I've seen them scurry from my food—
but I already know they favor
dark places, warm and damp,
and they are omnivores
who devour even their own dead skin.
My first memory of death
is large bugs crawling like miners
in and out of our pet chameleon's mouth.

SENSITIVITY TRAINING

A vacant cell
somewhere in Stillwater Prison:
I'm placed here alone
with instructions to strip to my shorts
and lie with my back on the floor,
which is cold like an empty tub.
What next? clangs the steel door.
A man, black, heavy,
wearing only trunks, a gold earring,
immediately lies on top of me,
face to face, body to body.
"How do you feel?" he asks,
settling his weight on my chest.
What next? clangs the steel door.
Another man, white, heavier,
his hairy skin wet with sweat,
flops on top of us.
"How do you feel?" he asks.
"Get the hell off!"
Delighted, they pull me up.
Doors and doors open before us,
and down a long corridor we chant,
"Say what you feel, say what you feel,
stiff upper lips are out of style,"
until they're gone suddenly like busy doctors,
and I'm driving, hurrying home,
my mind hot with confrontations
before the silver road turns gray.

SURPRISE PHONE CALL

"You're forty-one and better start," she said,
sounding concerned but also satisfied,
with her last child in school. What looms ahead,
I thought, as she divulged her tubes were tied.
Her second husband left. "It hurts, but, hey,
how about a bunch of us getting together?"
I said the old gang's gone, all moved away,
but really thought why mess with ominous weather.
She mentioned Chad, her son, a week ago
came home and swore he'd seen me on the street.
I couldn't tell: he's had twelve years to grow—
I'd see a stranger I'd hesitate to greet.
Maybe Chad passed me carrying his son,
recalling Mom's boyfriend who was no fun.

WISTFUL LIST

I should have kept in touch with her through friends
or called sometime, but after years her name
was added to a wistful list that wends
like a white streamer at a football game.
I spent my twenties as a bachelor
in furnished rooms I usually didn't lock,
and when I packed and moved, I took no more
than one carload. The rest I'd leave or hock.
Those young unending days flowed cheap as beer
chugged down and easily replaced as if
cases of it would always be ice cold and near
and empties could be tossed far off a cliff.
She spent her twenties married, having kids,
and would have thought my life was on the skids.

WHAT TO SAY

All night it's been a kind of peekaboo,
our distance longer than the barroom's length.
I should have greeted her and talked a bit
when she came in, but now she's joined some friends.
I'll say hello-goodbye when I go out.

At other times a face that looks familiar
pops out at me like a lost motorist
who yells, "Hey, bud, where's the courthouse from here?"
I'm usually in the street, cars revving up,
light changing green, and look away uncertain,
recalling seconds late what I should say.

But she is more than a familiar face:
the ex of a close friend. Their bitter end
made her go underground to break from him.
What would we talk about—the current weather,
a topic we'd deride those crazy nights,
all of us drinking, jabbering toward dawn.

"So how've you been?" I ask as I pass by.
She glances up expressionless. Her eyes
are masked in fingers clenched like pried white bars.
As if we'll never chance to meet again,
I call, "Take care, Eileen. Have a good life."

STAINED-GLASS LIGHT

"We're not at mass to have a merry time,"
Monsignor Mulligan admonished us.
"We're here to praise almighty God and thus
by prayer, not feeling good, reach the sublime."

Monsignor and the nuns commanded prayers.
In Lent our school was ordered to daily mass:
chaste troops to save from purgatory's morass
a sullied soul or even settle world affairs.

"God listens closely to His children's pleas."
They smiled and tacked on prayers because the Pope
feared Russia teetered us on a treacherous slope.
I thought of lunch, cartoons, and my sore knees.

My indignant father warned me senior year
if I enrolled at the U and not a Catholic school,
I'd scrutinize my faith like a molecule
and dismiss it all with my studied sneer.

But I'd already left, one afternoon in spring.
My adolescent faith cracked like lake ice.
I skipped from Stations of the Cross to paradise
outside as my classmates began mournfully to sing.

Noon hour from work, my mind and body tight,
I enter again the parish church to sit
in a dark pew, and though I feel like a misfit,
I am surprised by the vast stained-glass light

that beautifies the white pillars of stone
and the gold and silver leafwork finishing
the marble masonry. Unease diminishing,
I leave elated in my flesh and bone.

THREE

COMFORTING ARMS INSURANCE COMPANY

TO WHOM IT MAY CONCERN

I stand all day
and bone chickens.
I've done this for years—
dump the meat on one belt,
the bones on another,
to carry them away.
I'm only fifty-three,
but my feet are all sores
from diabetes and the floor
wet with running water.
My doc says to quit
while I'm still walking.

BREATHLESS

"I can't breathe.
I walk a block
and have to stop."

Lung
farmer
furrier
welder
lung
malt worker
bird breeder
mason
lung
coffee worker
silo filler
bark stripper
lung
glass blower
mushroom worker
miner
lung
black
vanishing
lung
emphysema
bronchitis
pneumonitis
silicosis
suberosis
anthracosis
asthma
lung
miner
mushroom worker
glass blower
bark stripper
silo filler

coffee worker
mason
bird breeder
malt worker
welder
furrier
farmer
lung
black
vanishing
lung

FROM THE PARKING LOT

Briefcase in hand, my lights and doors rechecked,
I launch my half-mile hike to work from here.
After a block I wonder if I hung
that blasted parking pass from the rearview mirror.
I'll get a ticket though I've parked there years.
Oh hell, I'm late and in full coffee stride,
my first cup managed on the drive. Some days
I'm fueled so high I coast on auto-glide.

This usual route is dangerously calm.
So early, six o'clock, traffic is light
like snow-filled streets after a stormy night,
a plow the only vehicle in sight.
Plunged deep in my dawn thoughts and walking fast,
I'd like someone to put me on alert,
pop out at me as in a video game,
scoring a cautioning point but no real hurt.

As if on cue, I'm stopped by a large bug
stalled on the service station's entranceway:
gray, very flat, a thousand writhing legs,
a creature truly uneasy with the day.
What else might be ahead to startle me?
One morning blood drops trailed from a dark bar.
Or will the portrait studio's window beam
the latest luminous high-school senior star?

CLAIMS EXAMINER

Decisional Review has firmly bounced
a case I've done, returning it to me
to do more work. I'm charged a major error—
enough of these and my job's in jeopardy.
The claimant's been denied six times before
for his sore knees. I find he's mentally ill
and grant him benefits back several years.
They want his starting date back further still.

I'm stuck and feel like the lanced pig Earl drew
on his DR return for a misspelling.
His comical depiction shook DR,
though Earl's intent was just to keep from yelling.
I take my lumps, not wanting to provoke
a prolonged searchlight on a future case,
as an escapee scaling the wall must fear
the field below will have no hiding place.

Developing the claimant's onset date
for disability twelve years ago,
I'll call three clinics where he might have gone,
then his ex-wife, who certainly would know
and might rehash details of strange behavior.
From him I'll need a list of all his work
and any friends. But, cripes, I'm swamped—my desk
is heaped with files, and, damn, here comes my clerk.

HER SCHEDULE UNRAVELING

You want to hear about my day so far?
Good! First, I had to reach day care by eight,
or Shawn would not be fed. My keys were lost—
at night she charges extra if you're late.
I found our spare, but then the car won't start,
and Jay's in meetings at the university.
I called my dad and woke him up to ask
what's plus and minus on the battery.

My neighbor jumped it. Then I needed gas,
five miles of freeway from the service station.
I sputtered in and filled it up but had
to tug Shawn—yanking was a real temptation—
from his car seat and lock the car to pay.
I left it on, afraid it wouldn't run.
Inside I phoned the day-care mom, who said
to hurry up—breakfast was almost done.

And now the combination on the door—
my keys were locked inside—had been wiped out.
With Shawny crying, one more thing I swear
to God I would've started to scream and shout.
I called the U and paged my husband there.
He sounded frantic coming to the phone,
then mad. Somehow he knew the special code,
informing me in his superior tone.

ABRAHAM, MARTIN, AND GEORGE

Once at a party an old friend complained,
"I thought I wouldn't have to think tonight,"
when car talk turned to economic views.
Right now that quip of his strikes me just right.
Spending lunch hour alone, I usually read,
eat lightly, and then walk around downtown.
I've got the choice to think or not to think
on days when excess work has weighed me down.

Today a columnist defends George Wallace,
frail, sick. It's twenty years since he was shot
and almost thirty since as Alabama's
blunt governor and self-styled patriot
he blocked black students from a schoolhouse door.
His blustery speech that day was meant to dull
the whetted rage of racist militants.
It worked, the writer claims, a miracle.

Claptrap like this will always make me think
how Medgar Evers died that night. Where's that?
And I remember twenty years ago
when on a coffee break four of us sat
deep in a card game when the radio blared
the shooting. "Damn the violence," I said.
My office mates, all black, glanced up at me.
Gwen spoke: "I hope the dirty bastard's dead."

JOSTLED

On a hot day I'm stopped at a long light.
An anxious car swerves into the right lane
to surge ahead when the red changes green.
His revving engine jostles my migraine.
Who does he think I am? Some pencil pusher
who drives a Ford and wouldn't dare exceed
in anything, even the posted speed?
He steps on it, but he can't gain the lead.

I flick my rearview mirror to blot him out,
then think of stopping to have a calm talk
and tell him that this street was once a trail
that pioneers would ride on horse or walk
for several days to buy supplies in town.
And if the store were bare of seed or salt,
they plodded home again, not sputtering blame:
how could the ice-clogged river be at fault?

I let him pass but watch him carefully
and try no triggering move like braking fast.
Pointing, he squints one eye like a marksman
taking dead aim. Who knows where he's been last?
Perhaps he's just been downsized from his job,
cleaned out his desk, and hit some downtown bar.
I slow way back, recalling last week's news:
a man found shot beside his idling car.

DAILY TAUNTS

At home a notice rattles Friday's mail.
An inspector states my sidewalk needs repair.
"Questions? Please call from 8:00 to 9:00 A.M."
Upset, I go outside to locate where.
Knowing I'll blow my stack all weekend long,
surely this Mr. Meyer enjoys a jest.
Compared to the slight rise I ascertain,
my neighbor's sidewalk is Mount Everest.

Like any home owner, I hardly want
the government plucked from my life for good.
Still, I now fantasize incisive schemes
to clear the nation of inane deadwood.
On Monday morning I phone him at eight.
"Sorry, Inspector Meyer is sick today."
No doubt he's fishing for walleyes up north
or playing golf. Tuesday I'll have my say.

On Monday claimants I've denied call mad.
"I know real pain. I wince lifting my son."
"I never had a fat chair job like yours.
I loaded trucks. I worked. It wasn't fun."
"All your smart gobbledygook I've got on tape."
On Tuesday I ask what Mr. Meyer wants.
I roar no lawsuit threats but learn the cost.
I'd feel absurd echoing daily taunts.

OFFICE BLUES

Our building's guards, Johnny and Jim, are gone,
have been replaced by cameras on each floor.
The monitoring staff that's always hiring
can't tell a tenant from a visitor.
In uniform and cap Johnny would shoo
loiterers like pigeons from the entryway,
while Jim with a nightstick would rouse stairwells
of lurking characters to earn his pay.

And Eddie's been replaced by a drop box
after eight years working the parking lot.
His statuesque presence was reassuring.
The lot's new owner blurts to me, "I'm not
about to pay some guy five bucks an hour
for little more than stand inside that shack."
Mornings I see him in the labor pool
but when I wave to him, he won't wave back.

With the first snow, my fender somehow smashed—
the unattended lot was still unplowed—
I crammed what happened in the shack's mail slot,
aware the damage would be disavowed.
Last week surveillance cameras scanned unwatched
as a bookkeeper trying to stay ahead,
working late hours for a computer firm,
was raped inside their ramp and left for dead.

SQUEEZE

The new examiners despise their jobs:
there's too much work, they want a cap on it,
and someone's chewing on them all the time.
One dreams she's flailing in a paper pit.
I offer at a special union meeting
that veterans like Earl and me could ease
their load by doing difficult dictations.
But that, they snap, would just suspend the squeeze.

"Damn, you don't get it," Rick says. "Hell, you're all
so whipped and hog-tied none of you can see
you've got to rock-and-roll around this place
or management will just do twiddly-dee."
Rick's new, a former welder from Detroit,
an activist in boots and ponytail.
He knows he's really shook our union rep
by needling that his left-wing talk is stale.

Around the room examiners murmur.
"Why is this unknown character," they ask,
"here just six months, deciding strategy?"
They look to Sid to take the guy to task,
but Sid, our rep, leans back, knows those in charge
fear Rick, a gritty idealistic cuss.
Though they've refused to meet with feisty Rick,
they will, without delay, sit down with us.

CUBICLES

Exchanging offices for cubicles,
we've turned a floor to modern modular space.
Though giving up the privacy of doors,
we've gained a windowed, open, light-filled place.
I thought the cubicles were cattle stalls
when stopping by before our move was made.
But now when I stand at my desk and see
a friend or sky outside, I like the trade.

Though piped-in white noise deadens sound,
I still hear voices muttering close by.
"My ex dropped in last night for you-know-what.
He wouldn't make a prick on a horsefly.
I gave it to him quick and sent him home."
Surely she senses I might overhear,
but, cognizant of cubicle etiquette,
she rattles on as if no one is near.

Later I stop outside her cubicle
and stare at the few things in view: a shell
necklace, a family photo without him,
a sign, "The best revenge is living well."
At home this space could be her special room
and I someone who pauses on the street,
daydreaming what the life inside is like.
Oh, here she comes—I hustle to my seat.

BREAKING POINT

A lawyer waiting to review a file,
a doctor calling on a claimant's case,
a Monday rush of work demanding now—
Meg hurries by me, tension on her face.
"I feel like when my dad raped me," she blurts.
I am as shocked as Meg by her remark.
We usually pass with "Hi" and "How's your day,"
expecting genial patter, nothing dark.

Flustered, Meg grips my hand and places it
beneath her breast. "I had a rough childhood.
My dad was sexually abused when young."
Her blurred words struggle to be understood.
Hoping she'll free my hand, I sympathize,
babbling lines like "I've heard that experts say..."
Eyes down, co-workers pass as if we're lovers
dallying in a public entryway.

I gently tug my hand, and Meg lets go,
smiling and then collapsing into tears.
I am a stranger at an accident,
unable to control how it appears.
Stepping toward her, I tell her she'll be fine
and hold her close, whatever it will take
to bring her calm, hoping real help arrives
to fix what's broken or about to break.

REMEMBRANCES

Today I'm passed a thin white envelope:
a woman in accounting's given birth.
I add a buck and forward it by hand,
as some may filch no matter what it's worth.
Or it could end up like Claire's envelope
that started out and never made it back,
a windup toy sent dutifully off,
found two weeks later on the coatroom rack.

Little was done for Jim DeNet's last day,
his resignation after fifteen years.
He did good work but jabbed at management.
A bunch of us at lunch took him for beers.
Later that day a summer temp received
a farewell party in our meeting room.
His supervisor raved about his skills.
Jim leaned in the far corner by a broom.

Another job, when I was twenty-two,
offered the Special Gift and Flower Fund.
Members received set gifts for such events
as births and resignations. I was stunned—
what phoniness—and told the chairman so.
I tried to make him mad by calling it
Ye Old Fixed Gift and Plastic Flower Fund.
He smiled and didn't push its benefit.

DEADLINE

The time Claire rode the bus a mere two blocks
to make our unit's picnic at Rice Park,
I thought she had arthritis in her legs.
Claire laughed as if it were a whim or lark.
Long thin legs balancing her barrel shape,
she hadn't seen a doctor in ten years.
He told her then to quit Pall Malls or else.
She turned to vitamins to treat her pains and fears.

Claire, the head secretary for our unit,
would herd her staff, steadfast as a sheepdog,
overseeing when clerks would come and go
and keeping typing to a small backlog.
Then, taking on the duties of a clerk
whose spot the tightened budget wouldn't fill,
Claire winced when picking up our mail and files.
Her office route became a long steep hill.

"I'm phoning now, before you go to work,"
my supervisor opened. "Claire got sick
late yesterday. She had a heart attack,
a massive one. It hit her like a brick.
Her cough was not her usual smoker's cough.
I said, 'Your hands look blue.' She said, 'I'm fine.'
I called an ambulance. Claire died last night,
mumbling, I'm told, about some damn deadline."

FLASH FIRES

Flash fires of anger have swept through the office.
An unnamed clerk has blamed our Unit J
for killing Claire. Her mother at the wake
said Claire's weight loss was noticeable each day—
couldn't we tell? And now who'll care for them,
her mother and two frail and failing aunts?
Claire, their attentive kin, would use vacation
to shop and cook, houseclean, and tend their plants.

Upset, our unit met with management.
A young assistant listened for half an hour,
acknowledging that Claire was overworked,
but then he counterpunched with swift grim power:
"Each worker should look out for Number One.
Claire had sick leave or could have transferred out."
Rising, he told us he reads history
when he's so stressed from work he'd like to shout.

Weeks later Claire's son Jackie still had not
picked up the box of things beside her desk,
now occupied: five pairs of shoes, breath mints,
a carton of Pall Malls. "How picturesque,"
I quipped, "'Last Lunch Encased in Tupperware.'"
"Okay, okay," my supervisor said,
"only Claire's vitamin man has ever come.
I'll move the box to the storeroom instead."

STILL HERE

Having been in and out of jobs for years
before I got this one, my dreams are bleak
of seeking other work. I see myself
at home, a winter afternoon, long week
ending. I haven't even checked the paper,
except for TV. My windows are shut,
my torpor sealed like a weatherized house.
I probe a week's advance in my beer gut.

This job I often rip has benefits.
I'm at my desk by six-fifteen, awake,
propped up perhaps, but here before the blare
of cars or squawk that stirring birds can make.
I take a walk at noon. I'm done at three,
prompt as a factory whistle changing crews.
I leave my work at work, so nights are mine
to read, bike, golf, whatever I might choose.

Tina, with whom I've lived for many years,
is self-employed. Her graphics work is rush.
She often toils late like a frazzled monk,
retouching images with a frantic brush.
If she could set her schedule, she would take
classes in tin whistle and modern dance.
But now her skills are threatened by computers,
so she takes all the work she has a chance.

RUSH HOUR

Flashing police-car lights a block away
converge upon the Jackson bridge, which spans
the freeway carved beneath. A figure perched
on top of the wrought-iron fence has plans,
it seems, to leap into the traffic below.
More than one death might happen if he did.
The cops approach with care as if he bites,
and now one calls, "Easy, son. Okay, kid?"

The man is slim with long blond hair. He looks
eighteen or so in black T-shirt and jeans.
A pirate's snarl glares gold on his black cap
as if to ward off any thugs or fiends.
Both life and death have contracts out on him.
His free-range days have dwindled down to this:
rush hour below, fierce as a flooding river,
or else some institutional abyss.

He looks confused like Luke, my old workmate
and brandy drinker who ends up at least
once a year held in hospital or jail—
three days last time till his delirium ceased.
I'm no help here. I head to where I park,
as the cops spread out near the fence. What plight
might Luke be in right now? I wouldn't know—
I haven't phoned in months. I will tonight.

ABOUT THE AUTHOR

Kevin FitzPatrick was born in Saint Paul, Minnesota, and was educated at the University of Minnesota and the College of Saint Thomas. He was the editor of the *Lake Street Review* from 1977 to 1991. About his first book of poetry, *Down on the Corner,* published by Midwest Villages & Voices, Meridel LeSueur wrote, "He is a wonderful chronicler of the people's journey." Besides magazines and newspapers, his poetry has appeared in anthologies, most recently in *Call Down the Moon: Poems of Music* (Margaret K. McElderry Books), *The Next Parish Over: A Collection of Irish-American Writing* (New Rivers Press), and *Ringing in the Wilderness: Selections from the North Country Anvil* (Holy Cow! Press). His poetry has been heard on "The Writer's Almanac" and "Weekend Edition" over Minnesota Public Radio and other public radio stations. He lives in Minneapolis, Minnesota.

MIDWEST VILLAGES & VOICES

PROSE

Every Woman Has a Story, edited by Gayla Ellis
Winter Prairie Woman, by Meridel LeSueur
Irene: Selected Writings of Irene Paull,
edited by Gayla Ellis et al.

POETRY

Payments Due: Onstage Offstage, by Carol Connolly
The Necklace, by Florence Chard Dacey
Heart, Home & Hard Hats, by Sue Doro
Down on the Corner, by Kevin FitzPatrick
Caravan, by Ethna McKiernan